Making Strategic Analysis Matter

Gregory F. Treverton, Jeremy J. Ghez

Prepared for the National Intelligence Council

NATIONAL SECURITY RESEARCH DIVISION

The research described in this report was prepared for the National Intelligence Council. The research was conducted within the RAND National Defense Research Institute, a federally funded research and development center sponsored by the Office of the Secretary of Defense, the Joint Staff, the Unified Combatant Commands, the Navy, the Marine Corps, the defense agencies, and the defense Intelligence Community under Contract W74V8H-06-C-0002.

Library of Congress Control Number: 2012934034

ISBN: 978-0-8330-5879-9

Published 2012 by the RAND Corporation
1776 Main Street, P.O. Box 2138, Santa Monica, CA 90407-2138
1200 South Hayes Street, Arlington, VA 22202-5050
4570 Fifth Avenue, Suite 600, Pittsburgh, PA 15213-2665
RAND URL: http://www.rand.org/
To order RAND documents or to obtain additional information, contact
Distribution Services: Telephone: (310) 451-7002;
Fax: (310) 451-6915; Email: order@rand.org

Preface

This research was conducted for the organization formerly known as the Long-Range Analysis Unit—now called the Strategic Futures Group—of the National Intelligence Council (NIC). Its aim was to concentrate on consumers of intelligence and ask how they might be better served by analysis whose focus is longer term or more strategic than the current reporting that dominates today's intelligence production. These proceedings report on a workshop, held on July 1, 2010, attended by distinguished current and former policymakers as well as intelligence officers. The list of participants is provided in Appendix B. Appendix A describes related project research conducted by the authors into how strategic analysis is done and presented in other domains of analytic activity.

This research was sponsored by the NIC and conducted within the Intelligence Policy Center of the RAND National Defense Research Institute, a federally funded research and development center sponsored by the Office of the Secretary of Defense, the Joint Staff, the Unified Combatant Commands, the Navy, the Marine Corps, the defense agencies, and the defense Intelligence Community. For more information on the RAND Intelligence Policy Center, see http://www.rand.org/nsrd/ndri/centers/intel.html, or contact the director (contact information is provided on the web page).

Contents

Figure and Tables

Figure

Tables

Key Workshop Takeaways

- The urgency of the immediate is a fact of life for policy officials, and so it is the intelligence community that must adjust. One way to do this is to continue to "push" strategic analysis even in the absence of much visible demand from the policy community.
- Because strategic analysis is iffy, contingent, and often future, it is easily dismissed by policy officials as a luxury or an irrelevance. The bar is high.
- Subtle marketing—as in the case of the NIC's *Global Trends* series—is valuable when it is possible. Policy officials may pay attention once the media does.
- The fact that the NIC is now responsible for preparing Principals Committees and Deputies Committees immerses the NIC in current intelligence but also provides its analysts, including those in the Strategic Futures Group, with an invaluable sense of what is on the policy agenda.
- Strategic analysis by analogy can be useful. Policy officials often reason that way, so intelligence can help them ask, for instance, "Does Plan Colombia offer insights for Afghanistan?" If the analogy is to be useful, it probably has to be framed in a way quite specific to the issues at hand—which again puts a premium on knowing the policy agenda.
- Looking for opportunities means reaching out to the "belly buttons" of strategic planning across the government. Those are more numerous now than in earlier years, and they have organized themselves. They are natural drivers and consumers of more-strategic analysis.
- Thinking about new ways of engaging policy officials is imperative. The "products" of strategic analysis may be people—the NIC's National Intelligence Officers, for instance, or the analysts who accompanied the President's Daily Brief briefers for more-strategic conversations with President George W. Bush—not papers. The NIC and other organizations have developed half-day games that let policy and intelligence jointly explore paths, policy options, and their consequences across time and for other issues.

Acknowledgments

Our greatest debt is to the distinguished current and former policymakers who attended the workshop or participated in interviews outside of the workshop. They were generous with their time and even more so with their insights. We also owe an intellectual debt to our formal reviewer, Paul Herman. Herman brought a trifecta of perspectives: participant at the workshop, long-time intelligence analyst doing strategic and innovative analysis, and now outsider observing from the academy.

Abbreviations

AIDS   acquired immunodeficiency syndrome

CIA   Central Intelligence Agency

DNI   Director of National Intelligence

EADS   European Aeronautic Defence and Space Company

HIV   human immunodeficiency virus

NATO   North Atlantic Treaty Organization

NIC   National Intelligence Council

CHAPTER ONE

The Purpose of Strategic and Long-Term Analysis

As one of RAND's best long-term planners, Jim Dewar, puts it, "If long-term thinking doesn't influence what you do today, it's only entertainment." These proceedings reflect on a workshop that brought together intelligence professionals and distinguished senior current and former policy officials to see how Dewar's test might be met: How do policy officials think they might be served or have been served by strategic analysis? In addition, several former senior policymakers who could not attend the workshop were interviewed separately. (Nothing was said for attribution, but those who attended the workshop or were consulted separately are named in Appendix B.) The Dewar test should not be taken too literally, for the result of strategic and long-term thinking need not be action; if the thinking leads to better understanding, it may result in deferring action, not initiating it.

We begin these proceedings with an examination of issues in strategic analysis. We then look at a specific case (the Greater Middle East) and conclude with suggestions about how to do better strategic analysis. Appendix A reports on a scan of how private sector organizations conduct what might be thought of as strategic analysis in their context and how that analysis connects to strategic planning.

Who would have been able to imagine in 1910 that a world war would lead to the demise of great empires, to the emergence of fascism and communism, and to a durable state of cold war in a bipolar world? Yet, today's decisionmakers grapple with shifts that are as tectonic: economic crisis, demographic changes, a dramatically evolved North Atlantic Treaty Organization (NATO) alliance, a Greater Middle East in revolution, and the fiscal challenges lying ahead, for instance. Yet, the U.S. government seems as unable to come to grips with these shifts now as were decisionmakers before World War I.

In large measure, policy officials are driven by their in-boxes, so, when long-run issues are brought up, the inevitable question is "What can—or, more likely, *must*—I do about this today?" If the answer is "nothing," then attention quickly turns to the immediate. Moreover, for its part, the intelligence community has not been able to nurture strategic thinkers. Most analysts are trained to look for measurable evidence and to struggle with alternative possibilities, but they are not always willing to venture beyond the facts and the level of policy description.

Yet, strategic analysis is a potentially powerful tool for policymakers. These proceedings sometimes use the term *strategic analysis* to include both strategic analysis and long-term analysis, but it needs to be recognized that the two, although kindred, are not identical. Strategic analysis is usually long-term in reach, but it need not always be: It sometimes locates choices in a wide but immediate context of other issues and their effects. The liabilities of the two different forms of analysis also differ: Long-term analysis may imply that consequences can be postponed, and strategic analysis may confuse consumers with too many moving parts. The goal of both is to **help policymakers** think strategically—that is, **integrate into their calculations the wider context or a longer time stream of information (or both).**[1]

Strategic analysis can help policymakers **broaden the range of possible futures and thus better manage uncertainty**. Too much focus on the immediate often drives out consideration of the trend lines. Long-term analysis can help by focusing on sources of uncertainty and by identifying a range of possible futures that policymakers could face. The analysis could help decisionmakers assess the robustness of courses of action across a wide set of future contingencies. **By definition, long-term issues are mysteries, not puzzles or questions that could be answered definitively if only we had access to information that is, in principle, available.**[2] This is also true of most strategic issues. Whether al Qaeda possesses fissile material is a puzzle. By contrast, mysteries are questions that cannot be answered with certainty. They are future and contingent. Will North Korea agree to cease its nuclear program? No one knows the answer, not even North Korean leader Kim Jong Il. It depends. The question is a mystery, not a puzzle.

In the case of mysteries, the comparative advantage of intelligence's secrets and its secret sources is reduced. Those secret sources can supply the missing pieces of puzzles, but framing mysteries in a way useful to policymakers depends more on expertise and method than on specific bits of information. The challenge of reaching consumers is also much greater, for, if secrets provide an answer to an immediate puzzle, the implication for actions may be pretty clear. By contrast, strategic analysis may appear to complicate policymaking, not simplify it. For its part, framing long-term mysteries risks producing an answer to a question no consumers are asking (even if they should). **Even at their best, neither strategic nor long-term analysis can provide "the answer," and so it is all too easy for harried consumers to put such analyses in the "I'd love to read that if I had time" category.** Framing mysteries should impel intelligence to seek experts, perspectives, and methods outside government: in academia, think-tanks, and the private sector. Indeed, the longer the time horizon is stretched, the less the purchase of secrets and the higher the premium on tapping expertise outside government.

The challenge is to tap this expertise in a way that demonstrates value to customers *now*. And, as Table 1.1 demonstrates, the cultures of policy and intelligence are very different. Although it may be a slight caricature, the table suggests that it is no surprise that intelligence often is poorly integrated in policy and all the more so when the intelligence is strategic or long term. It is clear that neither the pressures nor the proclivities of policy are likely to change dramatically. Thus, intelligence must adapt.

---

[1]   One workshop participant recalled that, before the end of the Cold War, getting a briefing on Islamic fundamentalism was very hard, in spite of growing evidence of links between terrorist groups in Turkey and the Soviet Union. It seemed that analysts did not know political Islam well. They had not done much of either strategic or long-term analysis. He wondered whether, if policymakers had had broader and long-term insights, the United States would be confronting the issues it confronts today in Afghanistan. Similarly, given the levels of distrust in the Middle East toward the United States, can the U.S. government continue to make policy without accounting for public opinion in that region? Strategic and long-term analysis can help policymakers integrate those attidues into their strategic calculations.

[2]   On the distinction between puzzles and mysteries, see Gregory F. Treverton, "Estimating Beyond the Cold War," *Defense Intelligence Journal*, Vol. 3, No. 2, Fall 1994; Joseph S. Nye, Jr., "Peering into the Future," *Foreign Affairs*, Vol. 77, No. 4, July/August 1994, pp. 82–93.

Table 1.1
Contrasting Intelligence and Policy Cultures

Intelligence	Policy
Focuses on "over there," foreign countries	Focuses on "here," policy process in Washington
Reflective, wants to understand	Active, wants to make a difference
Strives to suppress own views, biases, and ideology	Acts on strong views, biases, and ideologies, at least some of the time
Time horizon is relatively long	Time horizon is short; an assistant secretary's average tenure is about two years[a]
Improves analytic products with time	Wants assistance "yesterday"
Understands the complexity of the world, perhaps overstating it	Wants (and is wont) to simplify
Knows that sharp answers or predictions will be wrong; spells out scenarios and probabilities instead	Ideally, wants "the" answer
Tends to take the world as given: It is there to be understood	Tends to take the world as malleable: It is there to be shaped
Tends to be skeptical of how much U.S. action can affect the world	Tends to overstate what the United States (and policy itself) can accomplish
Works in an almost entirely written culture	Works in a culture that is significantly oral

[a] This is an estimate across the entire government. In the George H. W. Bush and Clinton administrations, the median tenure of cabinet officers was 2.5 years and that of the immediate subcabinet level was 2.3 years; one-quarter of officers served less than 18 months. For a nice summary, see M. Dull and P. S. Roberts, "Continuity, Competence, and the Succession of Senate-Confirmed Agency Appointees, 1989–2009," *Presidential Studies Quarterly*, Vol. 39, 2009, pp. 432–453. Although these numbers have not changed much over time, there are large variations across agencies and positions.

Virtually every review of intelligence analysis notes the increasing urgency of the immediate and the resulting preponderance of current intelligence, or reporting, at the expense of long-term analysis. Most such reviews lament that concentration on the current.[3] The blue-ribbon panel on weapons of mass destruction expressed such a concern and recommended that the intelligence community establish a center or other focal point for long-term analysis.[4] The George W. Bush administration accepted that recommendation and gave the National Intelligence Council (NIC) the task.

The NIC's Strategic Futures Group thus seeks to anticipate challenges for policymakers, without setting geographic or time boundaries. The unit focuses on long-term issues, such as access to water, transnational crime, democratization, and climate change. It also is the NIC's focal point for strategic gaming, and it recently held exercises related to post-2012 Iraq, Iranian nuclear weapons, a North Korean collapse, secession by south Sudan, and the future of Afghanistan. The Group reflects the judgment by the NIC, and perhaps the government as a whole, that policymakers do not pay enough attention to the convergence of

---

[3]   See, for instance, the following RAND studies: Gregory F. Treverton, *Next Steps in Reshaping Intelligence*, Santa Monica, Calif.: RAND Corporation, OP-152-RC, 2005; Gregory F. Treverton and C. Bryan Gabbard, *Assessing the Tradecraft of Intelligence Analysis*, Santa Monica, Calif.: RAND Corporation, TR-293, 2008.

[4]   See The Commission on the Intelligence Capabilities of the United States Regarding Weapons of Mass Destruction, *Report to the President of the United States*, Washington, D.C., March 31, 2005.

trends and to the emergence of strategic opportunities and risks. Analytically, the NIC's challenge is to build a focal point or seedbed for pushing out the horizons of analysis across the intelligence community. It surely does not want to create a ghetto for strategic and long-term analysis, one that will permit administrations to respond to criticism by saying, "Look, we're doing that."

CHAPTER TWO
Issues in Strategic Analysis

Because strategic analysis is often underappreciated in the rush of the immediate, **it needs to be "pushed" by intelligence because it will not be "pulled"—i.e., demanded—by policy.**[1] That focus on the immediate means that the bar for strategic analysis is high. What it produces is often difficult to prove or is deemed improbable: more science fiction than science. If a time traveler brought back a *Washington Post* from 2025, people looking at it in 2011 would dismiss it as an implausible forgery. Recall Henry Kissinger's comment about a staffer making an argument about the future: "He warned me but did not convince me." **If the analyst is looking to provide the policymaker with something new but not actionable, getting an audience will require analysis with a high degree of sophistication.**

That said, those practicing strategic and long-term analysis face practical and methodological obstacles, limits that can undermine the credibility of the assessments in the minds of policymakers. When strategic analysis portrays bad news—such as the strategic weaknesses in the U.S. position in the Middle East—it runs the risk of being dismissed as "declinist," as downplaying the capacity of the United States. It has to make the case carefully.

In particular, **strategic analysis needs, almost by definition, to be truly multidisciplinary.** That is, it must integrate all the dimensions of a single issue rather than treating each dimension separately, and this is as hard for intelligence as it is for academia. For instance, some workshop participants regretted that the economic dimensions of issues were rarely integrated and instead most often presented in a separate paragraph or text box. Intelligence tends to hire people for their specific expertise and does not bring in enough people with the breadth to do strategic analysis. Unhappily, **the current political context is not necessarily favorable to innovation in this realm**: With the failure of intelligence in the case of weapons of mass destruction in Iraq prior to the 2003 invasion, analysts seem to be increasingly reluctant to go beyond a description of the facts, thereby limiting the potential to improve long-term analysis.

Moreover, **strategic analysts are not held accountable for their assessments, and they sometimes generalize the lessons of a particular event or oversimplify complex dynamics on the ground.** To be fair, who would do the accounting? The managers of analysts have their own stakes, senior policy officials do not stay long in office, and a Director of National Intelligence (DNI) tradecraft office would not have a lot of credibility in this role. Analyses are often not updated when shocks modify the strategic landscape or even trigger changes that undermine the entire analysis. For instance, in the aftermath of the successful and failed

---

[1] James Bond and Q are the analogy. Bond never asks for them, but Q is always giving him fancy gadgets. Bond never pays attention to them, and they do not turn out to be useful for their intended purposes. However, they always turn out to be vital in the end. By the same token, strategic analysis may not be wanted or appreciated in the short run, but it can come in handy.

"color" revolutions in Europe, the intelligence community can help by identifying which long-range policies seem to work and which do not. The unhappy consequences of the revolutions in Georgia and Kyrgyzstan support a plea for greater humility. So do the unfinished revolutions across the Greater Middle East.

Similarly, **strategic analysts often encounter policymakers on more-even terrain than they realize**. That is especially the case when policymakers acquire a degree of strategic knowledge through their experience on the ground that analysts are hard-pressed to match. For example, President George W. Bush had a unique view of Tony Blair and of the Prime Minister's positions because the two men spent a lot of time together. In addition, the longer the range, the more the analysis hinges on (1) theory, ideology, worldview, or all three and (2) U.S. capabilities and policies.[2] The first set of factors can undermine the credibility of long-term analysis, and intelligence's shunning of matters domestic makes the community less useful. Strategic analysis cannot recommend policies, but it does need to take the United States—still the most important single actor in international politics—explicitly into account as a driver. That is new and uncomfortable for agencies steeped in the Cold War practice of *foreign* intelligence, but it is imperative.

Even when policymakers express an immediate need, analysts of long-range issues are often able to deliver only six to nine months later, when the topic has become irrelevant.[3] In other, smaller countries, the intimacy of intelligence and policy agencies makes communication easier. In the enormous, far-flung U.S. government, however, communication is harder. Furthermore, exchanges of officials across agencies and across the policy and intelligence communities are insufficiently widespread; seconding someone to another agency too often means sloughing off an unwanted officer.

---

[2]   To be sure, domestic politics is often decisive in shaping immediate policy.

[3]   One participant recalled that, when the Sino-Soviet relationship normalized, it became evident to him that the Soviets had a surplus of troops at the frontier with China. He wondered how the drawdown would occur but was never able to persuade the intelligence community that it would actually happen. It did occur two years after normalization.

CHAPTER THREE

A Provocative Example: U.S. Policy in the Middle East

The convulsions raging across the Greater Middle East in 2011 make the workshop's discussion a year earlier seem almost quaint, and that gap demonstrates just how hard long-term analysis is. In the view of one workshop participant, U.S. strategy in the Middle East rested on four major assumptions: (1) A two-state solution to the Israel-Palestinian issue is the right outcome, and failure to implement it will result in catastrophic consequences; (2) Iran's nuclear program is a bad thing from which a set of negative consequences will follow; (3) authoritarian regimes are likely to persist in Egypt, Iran, Saudi Arabia, and Syria; and (4) Turkey may not continue to be the secular country that it has been over the years.

The workshop did, however, stress that these assumptions should be tested in order to accomplish intelligence's main goal: narrowing the range of uncertainty for policymakers. Testing these hypotheses involves searching for ways to attack them. Would sanctions against Iran work? Have they worked in the past, and what were their effects? Similarly, why is a two-state solution better? Would the solution undermine terrorism by suppressing one of its talking points?[1] In the end, something is going to happen. There will be surprises. Can intelligence narrow the range of uncertainty about game changers? In other words, what might the 800-pound gorilla be? A net assessment is necessary to determine enemy reactions to U.S. plans at the macro level. In this respect, however, humility in the intelligence community's ambitions is appropriate. Looking back at assumptions about Indonesia, for instance, it would be hard to discover an analyst who claimed several years ago that the country would enjoy an open, secular, and democratic political system and annual economic growth of 4–5 percent.

Serious testing of assumptions would engage policymakers. Now, in practice, assumption testing means Central Intelligence Agency (CIA) red cell analysts arguing with each other. The odds of this drill narrowing uncertainty are low. If policymakers really valued intelligence, analytic material would prime U.S. diplomacy. Diplomatic trial balloons, for instance, might be the political equivalent of Cold War probes of Soviet air defenses: The United States could, for example, craft an initiative designed to elicit a response that would shed light on whether Libyan leader Muammar Qaddafi should be treated as a murderous psychopath or a loving but eccentric father figure.

Testing assumptions can also allow policymakers and analysts to **update their views, beliefs, and knowledge about the Middle East.** Indeed, sometimes the assumptions in the heads of different politicians are quite different. For instance, President George W. Bush believed that as long as there were authoritarian regimes in the region, there would be no peace

---

[1] As another participant pointed out, this is similar to RAND's approach of assumption-based planning, which consists of teasing out assumptions and then seeing which might be vulnerable and which could be buttressed or hedged.

between Arab countries and Israel. President Barack Obama's presumption—that Israel's actions and the lack of progress on peace endangered U.S. troops in Iraq—was quite different.

Another example is the extent to which economic variables play the role U.S. policymakers believe they play. Americans usually assume that countries that are probusiness and promarket will also be pro-American or, at worst, neutral. In the Middle East, Turkey is a case of a promarket economy that is not pro-American: The country has boomed economically, but favorable Turkish opinions of the United States have decreased from rare to appallingly rare, according to Pew surveys.[2] Prime Minister Recep Tayyip Erdoğan's popularity was off the charts in the aftermath of the Gaza flotilla incident in May 2010 because he was seen at home as standing up to the United States as well as Israel. Turkey is in many respects an outlier, but it still demonstrates the value of testing assumptions about the economic dimensions of issues.

In addition, testing these assumptions can be the starting point for **an opportunity analysis that can lead policymakers to explore alternative sources of leverage** (that influence neighbors, allies, and the like). Even a year ago, it was apparent that succession struggles were coming in Lebanon, Libya, and other countries and that they not only will drive outcomes but also may present significant opportunities or sources of leverage for U.S. foreign policy. Similarly, a key relevant question is "On whose side is time?" Can policymakers get an indication of the dynamics in the region to determine where the sense of urgency is? Decisionmakers need to adopt an approach that allows the United States to take advantage of crises. In this approach, when they seek to answer the questions of different players in the region and assess their respective positions, they can identify opportunities to pursue.

Regardless of U.S. choices, however, underlying forces will express themselves independently of, say, election outcomes (e.g., How constrained will whoever wins be? By what? What will the winner face in the short run?) And so perhaps it makes sense, **before testing assumptions, to try to understand the strategic environment and the underlying dynamics.** How will demographic trends affect civil society, the supply of and demand for oil, and developing economies? Before options are explored, a conversation on the meaning of these underlying forces can play a fundamental role in initial assessments.[3]

The Dewar rule suggests the need to adapt strategy over time as events reconfigure the long-term picture and as second-order effects influence outcomes in unexpected ways. In the extreme, there is an occasional paradox in the policy world: **It is sometimes necessary to try and fail before a successful outcome can be reached.** Sanctions against Iran are an example. Even if they do not work, they are still a necessary step; without them, China and Russia are

---

[2] Favorable opinions of the United States in Turkey fell from 52 percent in 1999–2000 to a record low of 9 percent in 2007 before enjoying a small jump to 17 percent in 2010. Turkey had the lowest U.S. favorability rating among countries surveyed, tied with Egypt and Pakistan. For a summary of the evolution of favorable opinions of the United States in the world, see The Pew Global Attitudes Project, "Obama More Popular Abroad Than at Home, Global Image of U.S. Continues to Benefit," web page, June 17, 2010.

[3] The current global economic crisis presents both dangers and opportunities because it has the potential to reopen the question that we thought we had solved in the 20th century: Is there an alternative to capitalism after the failures of Marx, fascism, and communism? The answer was never quite so sharp as Americans were tempted to believe because social democratic capitalism in Europe was a kind of third way. Now, however, there may be a fourth way emerging in China: a statist, promarket, and authoritarian model with no social safety net but no budget deficit either. Changes can occur quickly if people do not get their entitlements and if growth stalls. One priority lies in determining how the shifts in the Sino-U.S. relationship will affect perceptions of the fourth way. The same holds true for world trade and its mercantilist proponents. China enjoys a very flexible system with world-class industries. It is now able to build a natural gas pipeline in one-third of the time that it would take any Western country.

unlikely to face up to their responsibilities. Sanctions may be politically and ethically necessary, but the way they fail will also matter. In fact, testing assumptions can put the focus on the benefits (in this case, the possible changes in Chinese and Russian behavior, given particular paths and scenarios).

Similarly, **the shifting balance of power affects how actors behave and how events evolve.** One participant observed that most regional actors in the Greater Middle East, such as Turkey, Syria, and the Persian Gulf states, feel that the shift in their region is in Iran's favor, whether or not Iran proceeds to build nuclear weapons. As another participant argued, the global financial crisis and the prospect of new fiscal constraints are not stopping Iran. If the United States says that it will not let Iran go nuclear and Iran still acquires nuclear technology, the United States' loss in reputation will be amplified, all the more so given its looming fiscal constraints.

So, too, if the United States fails in finding a solution to the Israeli-Palestinian problem, it will be important to observe which party strikes the final blow. Perhaps the two-state solution is impossible, but the way the solution dies will matter and influence perceptions of the United States: Will the United States give up or will the push come from the Palestinian or Arab side? **If the window of opportunity on this issue is indeed closing, then it may be necessary to recognize that there is no solution at all.**

CHAPTER FOUR

Strategic Analysis and Policymakers

The challenges for strategic and long-term analysis are daunting. Yet, the Middle East case discussion evoked an analytic framework for that analysis, one that bears resemblance to assumption-based planning as developed at RAND.[1] For the purposes of strategic intelligence, that framework comprises four components:

- **Understand the strategic environment and underlying dynamics.** This is no mean feat, to be sure, for it incorporates demographic, economic, and political trends, along with the critical intersections of those trends.
- **Identify key assumptions that underlie U.S. policy.** This, too, is as much art as science, but the participant who identified assumptions related to U.S. policy in the Middle East provided an example of how this can be done.
- **Test those assumptions against the strategic dynamics, asking which might turn out to be wrong and in what ways.** Ideally, this testing would include "signposts": indicators or warning signals that can be used to reveal when the vulnerability of an assumption may be changing.
- **Reexamine U.S. influence and opportunities.** For intelligence, this does not imply recommending policy, but it does require asking both whether possible U.S. actions might shore up vulnerable assumptions and how a changing assumption might open opportunities for U.S. policy.

A review of practice in other domains, especially private business, is set out in Appendix A. Lest government intelligence agencies think other domains do better, one of our interlocutors summarized the private sector's practice of strategic analysis thus: "No one does it very well." The participant's review emphasized several points that help illuminate the special challenges intelligence agencies face:

- When the trends affecting outcomes are finite and the uncertainties are quantifiable—or can be assumed to be so—the long run can be "mathematized" through, for instance, present-value calculations. Finance and resource industries make use of these techniques.
- When a quantified approach is not possible, scenarios can help decisionmakers narrow the range of uncertainty. Shell is the name most associated with this approach, but Southwest Airlines used a variant to hedge against rising fuel prices.

---

[1] James A. Dewar, *Assumption-Based Planning: A Tool for Reducing Avoidable Surprises*, New York: Cambridge University Press, 2002.

- Another bridge between strategic analysis and strategic planning is accounting for the wider context, particularly in noting "breaking continuities"—those developments that are making existing policies unsustainable. Recent AIDS policy in Africa is an example because new cases are arising faster than they can be treated with drugs, no matter how cheap the drugs can be made.[2]
- Strategic planning uses strategic analysis to develop robust strategies and to hedge against undesirable contingencies. Examples of the latter range from familiar financial instruments—e.g., futures markets, hedges against foreign exchange risk—to more-debatable approaches, such as Asian countries' response to the regional financial crisis and Turkey's "zero-problems" foreign policy.

Strategic analysis is more daunting for intelligence than for the private sector. Corporations, for instance, tend to do it relatively narrowly in their specific industrial sector and in relation to their principal competitors. They also have some financial instruments for hedging against risk that do not really have counterparts in foreign policy. Presenting unpopular analysis to policymakers is no easy task in either the public or private sectors, but ideology is more likely to be involved in public policy than in business decisions. For instance, Secretary of State Colin Powell tried to get the Palestine Liberation Organization to be more constructive but got caught off by the U.S. administration. He did not have the green light to pursue his idea. How could **the intelligence community** have helped? It **should be relentless about presenting alternative futures**. As noted earlier in a footnote, although James Bond ignored them, Q's gadgets turned out to be useful for Bond, but usually not in the way Q expected. That is the first and perhaps most significant lesson for improving long-term analysis.

Looking for opportunities by reaching out to what one participant called "belly buttons" of strategic planning across the government will be crucial to enhancing the effectiveness of strategic and long-term analysis. Those belly buttons are more numerous now than in earlier years, and they have organized themselves. They are natural drivers and consumers of more-strategic analysis. One workshop participant suggested that there is a link between the United States' success over the past two centuries and its ability to manage long-range issues. This solid track record can help long-term analysis develop and further improve policies. This analysis is appreciated, especially by the military as it develops strategies and shapes forces for the long term.

Even in their day-to-day work, when policymakers look at specific issues, the analysis of trends and potential shocks can play a useful role. And although it can be challenging to identify pockets of interest in key agencies because strategic planning is often done under the radar, some leaders (including some currently in power) have placed a very high degree of importance on long-term analysis. Former Secretary of Defense Robert Gates is often mentioned as an example. President George W. Bush was also very interested in this type of work, and he allocated time for strategic questions six days a week during the President's Daily Brief. He was

---

[2]   As one report puts it,

> Maintaining the program in its current form means a cost to the U.S. that would grow each year by amounts that many health and government officials say are unsustainable, especially in the tough economy. Under the administration's new global health plan, which seeks to spend $63 billion between 2009 and 2014 on global health, the U.S. has slowed increases in funding for HIV/AIDS programs while devoting more dollars and attention to improving maternal and child health, attacking neglected tropical diseases and implementing other initiatives. (Betsy McKay and Robert Guth, "Global AIDS Fight Shifts Toward Prevention," *Wall Street Journal*, July 17, 2010)

interested in deep-dives and longer analyses as well as in meeting specific analysts one-on-one to discuss what was going on in Iran, for instance. At the working level, a kind of "kitchen cabinet" of planners and analysts of long-range issues is developing and includes many participants in the workshop.

Identifying these pockets of interest would allow intelligence analysts to engage with policymakers and allow all participants to look in the rearview mirror and decide whether the scenario that is discussed is something desirable, what to do about it today, and how to provide feedback to the appropriate decisionmakers. The recommendation that policymakers and strategic analysts should seek to better coordinate their efforts was a central leitmotif in workshop conversations. As one participant put it, **the products resulting from long-term analysis should be in the bloodstream of policymakers. They should be absorbed horizontally and vertically in the decisionmaking processes.** There are economies of scale that can be made, most notably by looking at other products and by incorporating the notes and observations of key actors, such as ambassadors and senior officials (as in the case of President George W. Bush and his knowledge of Prime Minister Blair). In addition, long-term analysis can provide a test for information that does not ring right, reinforcing doubts or changing opinions as a result. In this sense, the intelligence community should not be too ambitious, and it should primarily focus both on providing insights and validation and on trying to correct policymakers' erroneous preconceptions.

The fact that the NIC is now responsible for preparing Office of the Director of National Intelligence seniors for the meetings of the Principals Committee and Deputies Committee is a distinctly double-edged sword, for it immerses the NIC in current intelligence. Yet, it also provides NIC analysts, including those in the Strategic Futures Group, with an invaluable sense of what is on the policy agenda. That work makes it easier for strategic analysts **to accompany bad news with opportunities for shoring up failing assumptions or hedging against potential failure.**

In addition, **thinking about new ways of engaging policy officials in strategic analysis is imperative.** One insight is that because strategic analysis relies on expertise and judgment more than immediate evidence, often the "products" are people—the NIC's National Intelligence Officers, for instance, or the analysts who accompanied the President's Daily Brief briefers for more-strategic conversations with President George W. Bush—not papers. So, too, the NIC and other organizations, including RAND, have developed gaming techniques to economize on the time of policy officials. Half-day games, for instance, let policy and intelligence jointly explore paths, policy options, and their consequences across time and other issues. Those policy officials will attend, especially if they have been engaged in choosing the topics.

Subtle marketing is valuable when it is possible. The NIC's *Global Trends 2010* report was a notable achievement. It gathered people from outside. It influenced a whole series of strategic documents, such as the February 2010 *Quadrennial Defense Review Report* and multiple State Department and White House documents. It was used to stimulate a discussion with many key actors—a demonstration of the value of "marketing." Indeed, sometimes such strategic analyses have more impact indirectly, since primary consumers may feel they need to pay some attention once the product has been picked up in the media.

Some workshop participants provided concrete suggestions for making long-term analysis more useful. The analysis should focus even more on **identifying the root causes of the trends it discusses and on identifying milestones and events that would indicate whether the trend is indeed materializing.** By broadening views and focusing more on ranges and contexts rather than on specific scenarios, long-term analysis could produce thinking that is more creative, more appealing, and better written.

But, an additional lesson drawn from the workshop conversation is the need for humility. **The bar for strategic analysis is high, so failures will occur, and successes may be modest.** One discussant, for instance, thought that U.S. policy on the Baku pipeline that transports oil from central Asia to the Turkish coast had been a success and that cross-cutting analysis played a role in that success, especially by facilitating interagency cooperation. He thought that might be a model for a Nabucco pipeline that transports natural gas from Turkey to Austria.

That led to another lesson: the potential value of analogies. Policy officials often reason by analogy—how often has "no more Munichs" been invoked in the last 70 years?—so helping them do so creatively can be a task for strategic analysis. For instance, does Plan Colombia offer any insights by analogy for counterinsurgency in Afghanistan? If analysis by analogy is to be useful, it too probably has to be framed in a way quite specific to the issues at hand, which again puts a premium on knowing the policy agenda.

Training and good management of human resources are fundamental to doing better at strategic analysis. The intelligence community needs to develop analysts who are able to think about the broader context, the long run, and strategic consequences. The real challenge lies in acting and responding while maintaining a strategic advantage of five or six moves ahead. It is also very important for analysts of the long term to be confident in going beyond the evidence. They need to enable policymakers to make the right judgment call. In the long run, truly joint approaches to moving officers around would also make a big difference. Now, for instance, the CIA's Directorate of Intelligence tends to regard officers seconded, even to policy posts, as lost to the real work, which goes on at "home." The right view would be the reverse, thinking of those officials around the government as doing the work, with headquarters playing a supporting role. This latter perspective is, interestingly, the view of the Directorate of Operations.

Strategic Analysis: Lessons from Practice in Other Realms

Key Lessons

- When the trends affecting outcomes are finite and the uncertainties are quantifiable—or can be assumed to be so—the long run can be "mathematized" through, for instance, present-value calculations. Finance and resource industries make use of these techniques.
- When a quantified approach is not possible, scenarios can help decisionmakers narrow the range of uncertainty. Shell is the name most associated with this approach, but Southwest Airlines used a variant to hedge against rising fuel prices.
- Another bridge between strategic analysis and strategic planning is accounting for the wider context, particularly in noting "breaking continuities"—those developments that are making existing policies unsustainable. Recent AIDS policy in Africa is an example.
- Strategic planning uses strategic analysis to develop robust strategies and to hedge against undesirable contingencies. Examples of the latter range from familiar financial instruments—e.g., futures markets, hedges against foreign exchange risk—to more-debatable approaches, such as Asian countries' response to the regional financial crisis and Turkey's "zero-problems" foreign policy.

To help policymakers integrate into their calculations the wider context or a longer time stream (or both), strategic and long-term analysis aim to locate current choices in that longer time stream or in relation to other issues. This appendix reviews how organizations in both the private and public sectors do this kind of analysis. It first considers ways organizations frame the issues they face, especially how they identify opportunities and risk. Then, it turns to the counterpart of that horizon scanning, strategic planning. Strategic planning is perhaps less immediately relevant to the Strategic Futures Group, but it does shape what its customers will want from it and how they will use what they get.

Ways of Framing the Issues the Organization Faces

"Mathematizing" the Issue

Given the uncertainty surrounding both the effects of the broader context and the long-term trends that could influence outcomes, framing the issue is critical. When it is possible, framing consists of "mathematizing" the problem, of providing a straightforward and intuitive assessment of a strategy's long-term impact. This approach, often based on simulations, uses a single point estimate or a set of such estimates. The approach is possible when the number of trends affecting the outcome is either finite (or assumed to be) and when the uncertainty surrounding these trends is quantifiable (or assumed to be). The resulting analysis provides decisionmakers with a point estimate that some industries consider sufficiently robust to use as the basis for their final assessments.

Examples

- **Valuing financial assets.** The most straightforward pricing method consists of discounting the future cash flows that the asset is expected to generate with the relevant interest rate so as to obtain the asset's present value. In this framework, discounting the expected earnings allows investment managers to account for inflation and the opportunity cost of money.[1] To enrich investment strategies through long-term analysis, analysts use the present as the benchmark with which all decisions are compared. In addition, this model assesses expected earnings in a probabilistic matter, given a wide range of assumptions about the firm's current and future environment and performance. Other models rely on a comparison between similar firms or similar sectors to test the robustness of the assumptions and the accuracy of the estimates. The prices of financial options—such as puts and calls—are also indicative of market expectations about earnings and are used in more-sophisticated valuation models. However, this framework assumes relative continuity in the firm's future environment and thus does not integrate well the risk of an exogenous and unpredictable shock, whether positive or negative. It also does not deal well with radical uncertainty and catastrophic risk.[2]

- **Determining resource reserves.** A second example is oil companies. For them, the most common long-term task is estimating the size of the reserves available—a proxy for future cash flows—in order to determine the viability of investments and to improve current strategies.[3] The industry also associates likelihoods with these estimates by distinguishing between proven and unproven reserves. As a result, companies and the industry as a whole are able to adopt a quantified approach to the issue that resembles the approach of financial asset valuation. It is noteworthy, however, that the Society of Petroleum Engineers' definitions of *proven* and *unproven reserves* factor the political and operational context into the probability that reserves will be recovered.[4]

---

[1] For a detailed explanation, see Robert C. Higgins, *Analysis for Financial Management*, eighth edition, Boston: McGraw-Hill, 2007, Chapter 7; Zvi Bodie, Alex Kane, and Alan Marcus, *Investments*, New York: McGraw-Hill, 2004, pp. 414–428.

[2] This argument has been repeatedly used to explain the trigger and dynamics of the 2008 financial crisis. Heavy reliance on the "value-at-risk" model led financial institutions to estimate their risk exposure for a given probability, but not beyond the predefined probabilistic threshold. For instance, an institution could estimate the maximum loss it could suffer with a 95- or 99-percent probability, but it would have to assume that probability distributions for future events could be inferred from past observations and ignore the probability of catastrophic or systemic risk. See, for instance, Aider Tuner, "The Uses and Abuses of Economic Ideology," Project-Syndicate.org, July 15, 2010; Joe Nocera, "Risk Mismanagement," *New York Times*, January 4, 2009.

[3] For instance, British Petroleum makes some of its estimates public on its website. See British Petroleum, "Statistical Review of World Energy," web page, June 2010.

[4] The Society of Petroleum Engineers defines *proved reserves* as

> those quantities of petroleum which, by analysis of geological and engineering data, can be estimated with reasonable certainty to be commercially recoverable, from a given date forward, from known reservoirs and under current economic conditions, operating methods, and government regulations. . . . If probabilistic methods are used, there should be at least a 90% probability that the quantities actually recovered will equal or exceed the estimate.

The society indicates that "unproved reserves are based on geologic and/or engineering data similar to that used in estimates of proved reserves; but technical, contractual, economic, or regulatory uncertainties preclude such reserves being

Recent events make including the political and operational context all the more crucial: Although exploiting oil has always been inherently risky, recent trends have compounded the challenges that the industry faces.[5] Heightened concerns about the environment throughout the world—not only in developed economies—are likely to lead to stricter regulations and standards that will make oil drilling more costly. This same is likely to be the case for insurance premiums and costs associated with maintenance.[6] In this context, a quantified approach needs to account for the significant political risk associated with the activity by integrating into the analysis the probability that the reserves in question will be recovered. These developments take the analysis into the next form of framing, risk governance. However, the quantified approach will remain the most prevalent form of long-term analysis in the oil industry.

Risk and Opportunity Assessment

The process of conducting risk assessments is not very different from efforts to value future profits, but risk assessments are more concerned with estimating the level of risk exposure than with determining future values. In their most generic form, risk-exposure assessments estimate a loss function that accounts for the magnitude of the potential losses and the probability that these losses will occur. Because this approach is risk-centered, it can involve a wide set of scenarios of potential losses and thus, unlike the valuation of a financial asset, does not focus solely on the generation of a single flow. The assessment can account for direct sources of risk (i.e., to which events the activity is vulnerable) and for second-order sources (i.e., what type of events could indirectly affect the ability to carry out these projects).

This approach allows analysts to differentiate between both the various types of risks and the diverse potential losses to which an organization may be exposed. This enables an organization to elaborate strategies to hedge against the different types of risk it faces. More-recent studies in risk analysis have featured the notion of *risk governance*, which involves a broader approach to risk—one that includes risk evaluation and characterization, risk management, risk assessment, risk appraisal, and communication.[7] However, as is true for discounting, this framework is also vulnerable to "black swans"—extreme scenarios that cannot be taken into account in the model.

The opportunities and the threats that are likely to matter most are often those that are rare and perhaps fleeting, that may arise from the simultaneous emergence of several win-

---

classified as proved." They are considered *probable* reserves when they "are more likely than not to be recoverable" and are considered *possible* reserves when the probability of recovery is less than 50 percent. See Society of Petroleum Engineers, *Glossary of Terms Used in Petroleum Reserves and Resources Definitions*, undated.

[5] In particular, one reports notes that

> most accessible and productive oil fields, including those in the Middle East and Russia, are now owned and operated solely by national oil companies. Leading international oil companies . . . therefore find their access to "easy" reserves rapidly shrinking. Indeed, it is the need for better equity positions in oil exploration and production that has driven the oil majors to look farther afield to higher-risk, more remote, more difficult-to-reach places, such as the deep sea, central Africa, and the Arctic. And as the availability of "bookable" reserves continues to diminish, the pace of growth and the earnings of the major oil companies will likely suffer even more." (Viren Doshi, Hege Nordahl, and Adrian del Maestro, "Big Oil's Big Shift," Strategy-Business.com, August 2, 2010)

[6] Doshi, Nordahl, and del Maestro, 2010.

[7] See, for instance, International Risk Governance Council, *White Paper on Risk Governance: Towards an Integrative Approach*, Geneva, 2005.

dows of opportunity or vulnerability.[8] The ability to account for the broader context and to go beyond isolated variables, to monitor major trends and to understand how these are likely to converge and influence outcomes, is fundamental to an organization's success in taking advantage of opportunities and protecting itself from emerging threats.

Examples

- **Constructing buildings in earthquake-prone areas.** The simulation of earthquakes and the assessment of their potential effects on buildings is a relatively easy task, given that seismic activity is naturally bounded and that engineers can infer the maximum size of an earthquake from previous observations. When the location and likelihood of seismic activity are known, managing the earthquake-related risks fits well with the risk assessment model. In particular, these simulations allow earthquake engineers to build structures that are robust across a wide set of earthquake scenarios, including seismic activity that would be "off the charts."[9]

  To be sure, other parameters influence outcomes. This explains why an earthquake of greater magnitude in Chile killed far fewer people than a smaller earthquake in Haiti at the beginning of 2010. In particular, the broader political context and the ability of the government to fund the appropriate infrastructures play a fundamental role by making some regions more vulnerable and therefore riskier, even in the case of similar seismic activity.[10] In that sense, constructing buildings in earthquake-prone areas is a typical long-term issue: one with negative outcomes that may or may not occur in the future on an uncertain scale that may be influenced by the broader context, including geography, politics, and governance.

  However, organizations that perform best seem to be those that are acutely aware of both risks *and* opportunities in their strategic landscape. Being obsessed with risk in any early-warning process or strategic environment assessment can often lead organizations to overlook opportunities. Competitors may seize them, gaining a leg up on organizations that fail to recognize them. An ability to conduct sensible long-term analysis often equates with the capability to understand the underlying dynamics of the market.

- **Google 20-percent time.** The Google organization provides its programmers with the incentive to adopt a more-experimental approach than they might in other firms or settings. Annually, programmers are allowed to use 20 percent of their time to concentrate on innovative ideas that could be good for the company or good for the world. Based on the academic ethos of the company's founders, in which the freedom to experiment is central, Google 20-percent time has allowed the firm to link the creativity of its engineers with the practical challenges and the strategic gaps of the firm's market. This approach allows the firm to be a proactive vector of change in an industry whose dynamics are

---

8   See, for instance, Donald N. Sull, "Strategy as Active Waiting," *Harvard Business Review*, September 2005, pp. 120–129.

9   A group of researchers at the University of Michigan was able to accomplish this feat by putting together a building structure that was able to resist greater seismic activity than that generated by a typical earthquake. See Science Daily, "New Building Design Withstands Earthquake Simulation," web page, March 9, 2009.

10   G .F. Panza et al., "Advanced Seismic Hazard Assessment," *Pure and Applied Geophysics*, Vol. 168, August 4, 2010, pp. 1–9.; John D. Sutter, "In Search of an Earthquake-Proof Building," CNN.com, March 2, 2010.

uncertain rather than an organization subject to the constant need to adapt to market forces.[11]

- **Visa and early warning.** In the late 1990s, Visa International implemented an early-warning system that tracked changes in the firm's strategic landscape and provided the firm's executives with a better grasp of how trends were converging. Similarly, a major actor in the telecommunications industry implemented a system that favored information exchange among the company's employees, who were then able to report what they were observing on the ground. Creating scenarios is not enough for companies that seek to maintain a strategic edge and to acquire greater awareness about the reality of their strategic landscape (and, therefore, about the scenarios that are in fact materializing).[12]

- **IBM and continuous renewal.** IBM has developed an alternative approach based on continuous, incremental, and strategic renewal of its activities accomplished through small and frequent investments from which it can learn.[13] This process allows the company to identify emerging business opportunities without increasing its exposure to risk. As a report indicates, "IBM made 25 'business bets' in the 1999–2004 period; three of these failed, but the remainder created more than $31 billion in additional revenue."[14] In addition, and perhaps more importantly, this process allowed the company's management to clarify its strategy to the company's employees and shareholders.[15]

- **Cisco and crowd sourcing.** Risk and opportunity analysis can also involve widening the scope of the analysis to think outside the box. For instance, in 2007, Cisco launched the I-Prize initiative, an external innovation competition in which outside individuals could offer their ideas on the new billion-dollar business. This allowed Cisco to validate some investment decisions it had already made and to reach "a worldwide audience of smart, passionate people eager to help . . . [it] drive innovation."[16] The company's initiative presents another variation of the early-warning approach to risk and opportunity analysis: Ideas out in the public but unknown to organizations can confirm initial intuitions or provide better insights than the ones already at hand.

- **Amazon and institutionalized horizon scanning.** Strategic thinking—the willingness and ability of an organization's management to encourage its executives and leaders to engage more systematically in long-term analysis—is decisive. Amazon's decision to create a team that can stay "abreast of what the company is working on and [that] delves into strategy issues" is illustrative of this need.[17] Thanks to weekly four-hour meetings and one or two two-day yearly meetings, the team is able to explore topics that are not press-

---

[11] See, for instance, Stephen J. Dubner, "Reading, Rockets and 'Rithmetic," podcast, Freakonomics.com, October 21, 2010.

[12] Leonard Fuld, "Be Prepared," *Harvard Business Review*, September 2003, pp. 20–21.

[13] J. Bruce Harreld, Charles A. O'Reilly III, and Michael L. Tushman, "Dynamic Capabilities at IBM: Driving Strategy into Action," *California Management Review*, Vol. 49, No. 4, pp. 21–43.

[14] Rajshree Agarwal and Constance E. Helfat, "Strategic Renewal of Organizations," *Organization Science*, Vol. 2, No. 2, March–April 2009, pp. 281–293; David A. Garvin and Lynne C. Levesque, "Meeting the Challenge of Corporate Entrepreneurship," *Harvard Business Review*, Vol. 84, No. 10, pp. 102–112.

[15] Agarwal and Helfat, 2009.

[16] See Guido Jouret, "Inside Cisco's Search for the Next Big Idea," *Harvard Business Review*, September 2009, pp. 43–45.

[17] Julia Kirby and Thomas A. Stewart, "The Institutional Yes," *Harvard Business Review*, October 2007, pp. 75–82.

ing or driven by the short run, to discuss these issues at length, and to make one or two strategic decisions.[18]

Using Scenarios to Narrow the Range of Possible Futures

When the level or nature of the uncertainty makes a quantified approach impossible or unreliable, many organizations, including intelligence agencies, adopt scenario-based approaches. The main goal of these approaches is to provide a clearer frame for the issue by narrowing the range of possible futures that decisionmakers are likely to face. Rather than predicting or forecasting, scenarios provide a series of alternative and usually mutually exclusive futures involving the issue at hand. Considering a set of scenarios often helps decisionmakers assess the robustness of their strategies across a wide set of possible futures. Those decisionmakers might, for instance, shape hedging strategies to limit exposure to a type of risk to which the organization is particularly variable.

Example

- **Shell and oil prices.** Shell's effort over the past 30 years to provide documented energy scenarios is perhaps the most famous implementation of this approach. Shell defines a scenario as a description of "alternative views of the future" that "identifies some significant events, main actors and their motivations, and . . . convey[s] how the world functions." Shell uses these scenarios "to explore possible developments in the future and to test [the company's] strategies against those potential developments."[19] In its 2050 edition, Shell identifies two major scenarios for the future of energy: Scramble and Blueprints. In the first, "policymakers pay little attention to more efficient energy use until supplies are tight. Likewise, greenhouse gas emissions are not seriously addressed until there are major climate shocks." In the second, "growing local actions begin to address the challenges of economic development, energy security and environmental pollution. A price is applied to a critical mass of emissions[,] giving a huge stimulus to the development of clean energy technologies, such as carbon dioxide capture and storage, and energy efficiency measures. The result is far lower carbon dioxide emissions."[20] Both scenarios have strategic consequences for businesses and policymakers seeking to hone their strategies in an uncertain environment. Taken together, these scenarios concisely describe the range of possible futures that decisionmakers will face, and they offer potential for improving the framing of long-term issues.

Identifying Paradigm Shifts

Strategic analysis can provide decisionmakers with a better grasp of ongoing paradigm shifts that are likely to create strategic ruptures. Understanding how shifts in the strategic land-

---

[18] Kirby and Stewart, 2007.

[19] Shell, "What Are Scenarios?" web page, undated. The page adds,

> As they identify discontinuity as a central issue for organizations, scenarios help businesses and governments to prepare for "surprising" change. An organization that is open to change is much more likely to survive and thrive than one that is continually chasing events. Good scenarios are ones that explore the possible, not just the probable—providing a relevant challenge to the conventional wisdom of their users, and helping them prepare for the major changes ahead. They will provide a useful context for debate, leading to better policy and strategy, and a shared understanding of, and commitment to actions.

[20] Shell International BV, *Energy Scenarios to 2050*, 2008.

scape and the balance of power affect traditional economic and political paradigms can help policymakers adapt to their new environment.

Examples

- **Power politics and new powers.** The changing political calculus of such countries as Brazil, China, and Turkey suggests that countries that have enjoyed high economic growth rates are increasingly looking to draw benefits from their strong economic positions and questioning the legitimacy of the current international political system. This shift has affected the traditional balance of power, bringing about changing preferences and priorities, new protagonists, and evolving outlooks on the issue of nuclear technology, for instance.[21]

- **A shifting balance of power.** What will the evolving strategic landscape and the current financial crisis entail for the future of economic—and, in particular, fiscal—policies? In the wake of the Asian crisis in the late 1990s, key players in the region accumulated massive currency reserves to help them better weather the next crisis. China, for instance, accumulated a sizable trade surplus, especially vis-à-vis the United States. The extent to which Chinese trade surpluses provide Beijing with increased leverage in the international sphere has been a recurring question in this context and points to a major risk entailed by this paradigm shift.[22] Lawrence Summers' characterization of the Sino-U.S. relationship as driven by a "financial balance of terror" suggests that the new economic deal is substantially modifying the traditional balance of power.[23]

- **Misunderstanding a paradigm shift can potentially lead to overreaction as well.** For instance, the attacks of September 11, 2011, placed al Qaeda at the center of foreign policy debates in the United States. The organization continues to receive substantial attention. That is true despite the fact that the 9/11 attacks that occurred ten years ago were by far the deadliest of its attacks. Figure A.1 displays the number of fatalities involved in al Qaeda attacks and the number of al Qaeda–related press articles in major world publications (which exceeded 6,000 annually between 2002 and 2008) between 1995 and 2009. This information suggests that the public's ability to update beliefs regarding the centrality of al Qaeda is poor.[24] More generally, the conclusion that a paradigm shift is occurring should not be based on a mere extrapolation of a trend. The 9/11 attacks may have been the most dramatic event that al Qaeda was able to trigger rather than an indication of its current and future strike capabilities. In the same way, a dramatic foreign

---

[21] See, for instance, Ian Lesser, "Turkey, Brazil, & Iran: A Glimpse of the Future," *Real Clear Politics*, May 21, 2010; Ivan Watson and Mitra Mobasherat, "Turkey: Iran Nuclear Swap Offer Shows 'Vision,'" CNN.com, May 18, 2010.

[22] See A. Evans-Pritchard, "China Threatens 'Nuclear Option' of Dollar Sales," *Telegraph*, August 8, 2007. For a contrarian view, see Daniel W. Drezner, "Bad Debts: Assessing China's Financial Influence in Great Power Politics," *International Security*, Vol. 34, No. 2, Fall 2009, pp. 7–45.

[23] Lawrence Summers, "Reflections on Global Account Imbalances and Emerging Markets Reserve Accumulation," speech, Reserve Bank of India, Mumbai, March 24, 2006.

[24] The organization's attack on the USS *Cole* in 1998 did not lead observers to consider the emergence of this new actor. Conversely, the scope and effect of the 9/11 attacks led to the extrapolation of the trend and to the widely shared belief that the confrontation between the United States and al Qaeda would be a defining one in the new century. Reports of turmoil within the organization and the dramatic decrease of fatalities linked to al Qaeda attacks seem to have a fairly limited effect on the centrality of al Qaeda as an organization.

Figure A.1
Al Qaeda–Related Citations in the Press and Fatalities Due to al Qaeda Terrorism

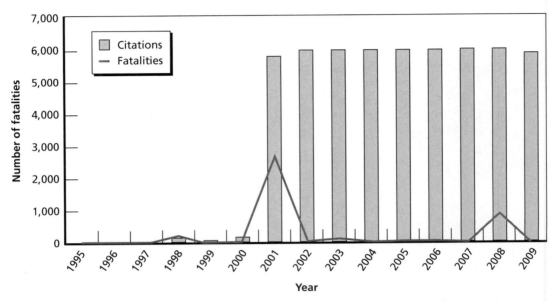

SOURCES: The numbers of fatalities triggered by an al Qaeda attack are drawn from RAND Corporation, "Database of Worldwide Terrorism Incidents," web page, no date available. The numbers of citations in the press are drawn from the LexisNexis Academic database "Major World Publications" category.
NOTES: The number of citations accounts for two spellings: "Al-Qaeda" and "Al-Qaida." LexisNexis was unable to generate an exact number of cites between 2002 and 2008 because there were more than 3,000 citations annually for each spelling. The number of references in those years should therefore be understood as exceeding 6,000.

RAND *CF287-A.1*

policy shift in such a country as Turkey may be more illustrative of an effort to rebalance a policy than a signal of other dramatic changes to come in the future.

- **Paradigm shifts also matter domestically.** An example is the debate over economic stimulus in the United States. Proponents of Keynesian economics argue that cutting back on government spending will doom any recovery prospects. Believers in the Ricardian equivalence proposition, however, argue that spending cuts will increase consumer and business confidence in the future and encourage economic growth.[25] Some reports have already pointed to changing consumption habits on the part of U.S. households, which have dramatically increased their saving rates since the beginning of the financial crisis in 2008.[26]

Understanding these paradigm shifts plays a fundamental role in the success of economic policies which rely, by nature, on long-term analysis. These paradigm shifts not only affect the broader context in which policies are implemented but may also influence outcomes in novel ways. As a result, these paradigm shifts, too, present both opportunities and risks.

[25] For more on this debate, see Barry Eichengreen, "Fiscal Fibs and Follies," Project-Syndicate.org, July 13, 2010; Paul Krugman, "Now and Later," *New York Times*, June 20, 2010; David Brooks; "Prune and Go," *New York Times*, June 10, 2010; Robert Skidelsky, "Keynes Versus the Classics: Round Two," Project-Syndicate.org, October 10, 2009.

[26] David Leonard, "The New Abnormal," BusinessWeek.com, July 29, 2010; Daryl G. Jones, "Personal Savings Rate: Worse Than We Thought," Money.CNN.com, June 30, 2010.

Accounting for the Broader Context: "Breaking Continuities"

Another bridge between horizon scanning and planning is accounting for the wider context. In particular, what might make a current policy unsustainable in the long run, even if it may be working and efficient in the short run? In the case of these "breaking continuities," changes are inevitable, though their timing is often hard to predict. Accounting for the broader context helps decisionmakers get a better grasp of the change that may be needed. It also allows an organization to avoid defining its issues in such narrow terms that it misses other opportunities or fails to identify other threats.

Examples

- **Allocating resources in the fight against AIDS.** Two distinctive features of the broader context, the global recession and the need to attend to other diseases, shape the environment in which the fight against AIDS takes place and are likely to affect the fight's efficiency. Recent reports have suggested that the current program, a priority of the George W. Bush administration, may be unsustainable in its current form. For instance, for every two people in Africa who start treatment, an additional five others on the continent become infected.[27] The fact that there are more infected people to treat, that treatment costs more and more, and that there is a need to allocate greater resources to other neglected diseases has forced a shift toward a greater focus on AIDS prevention.[28] The July 2010 international AIDS conference in Vienna confirmed this shift at the international level, especially in a context of the global recession and greater economic pressure on the major donors.

- **Changing business environments.** Similar breaking continuities affect the sustainability of business and organizational models in the face of changing regulations, different public and political perceptions, or an evolving strategic landscape. The ongoing shift in the business model of oil majors is an example. It results from greater public awareness and changing political demands vis-à-vis an activity that is increasingly considered risky. Although the past strategies of oil majors were lucrative, these changes require new policies. Similarly, low productivity rates and significant research and development costs have stirred a debate about the future of the pharmaceutical industry's business model, which faces less of a political risk than a long-term economic one. Suggested changes include public and prize-based funding of research and greater collaboration among the industry's companies to promote economies of scale.[29]

---

[27] Catherine Vincent, "Au Cameroun, la décentralisation du traitement contre le VIH est efficace [In Cameroon, Decentralizing the Fight Against AIDS Is Efficient]," *Le Monde*, August 14, 2010.

[28] As one report puts it,

> Maintaining the program in its current form means a cost to the U.S. that would grow each year by amounts that many health and government officials say are unsustainable, especially in the tough economy. Under the administration's new global health plan, which seeks to spend $63 billion between 2009 and 2014 on global health, the U.S. has slowed increases in funding for HIV/AIDS programs while devoting more dollars and attention to improving maternal and child health, attacking neglected tropical diseases and implementing other initiatives. (McKay and Guth, 2010)

[29] One commentary argues that

> the most effective pharmaceutical companies will be hubs at the center of a network of collaborators and suppliers, focusing internally on their core competencies, which might include medicinal chemistry, execution of clinical trials, or sales and marketing. They will facilitate interactions across their network to stimulate the development of innovation ecosystems. The resulting opportunities to expand beyond traditional products and markets will enable pharmaceutical companies to

- **Breaking continuities and organization.** Cisco offers another example of a breaking continuity that shaped the organizational model of the company. In the wake of ongoing market transitions, Chief Executive Officer John Chambers and the company's leadership implemented a collaborative management approach to tackle Cisco's most pressing challenges. This approach involved a more horizontal structure, the use of social networks and collaborative boards within the company, and the extensive use of videoconferencing to promote flexibility and quick reaction. As Chambers himself put it, "This companywide, council-based leadership model has allowed us to move from taking on only one or two cross-functional priorities a year in the past to addressing 22 this year. We think this is what organizations of the future will look like and that this 21st century leadership style will be a major competitive advantage for us over the next decade."[30] Identifying a breaking continuity can provide an organization with a strategic edge if it is able to implement effective change quickly and appropriately.
- **Not framing the issue too narrowly.** MasterCard's strategy in the wake of the economic crisis has consisted of attempting to enlarge the pool of potential clients who do use credit cards rather than trying to woo customers away from MasterCard's major (and dominating) rival, Visa. Through the creation of new products designed for a wide array of customers, MasterCard has sought to "grow the pie" and adapt to the new strategic landscape in which creditworthiness plays a more decisive role.[31]

Planning Strategically for the Future

The second broad family of techniques, strategic planning, allows policymakers to define a trajectory or set of trajectories for the organization, given the organization's resources and the external environment in which it operates. Strategic planning is in that sense the logical counterpart of horizon scanning or strategic analysis. The organization's mission is the major underlying driver of strategic planning, and it defines a major goal or set of goals. The organization's leaders implement a strategy or set of strategies that can help the organization accomplish those goals. Defining a series of actions helps the organization's leaders implement these strategies. Strategic planning thus takes strategic analysis of the external environment and adds to it the critical features of the organization. From this perspective, if strategic analysis accounts well for the broader context, it then allows the organization both to develop strategies that are robust across a wide range of futures and to hedge against undesirable contingencies.

---

evolve into companies that offer a range of health-care solutions. These will include not only prescription medicines, but also diagnostics, branded generics, and technologies that support personalized medicine . . . . (Jackie Hunter, "Open-Source Pharmaceuticals?" Project-Syndicate.org, July 29, 2010)

[30] Bronwyn Fryer and Thomas A. Stewart, "Cisco Sees the Future: An Interview with John Chambers," *Harvard Business Review*, November 2008, pp. 72–79. At the time, however, neither Cisco nor other companies were able to offer proof that horizontal networking, enabled by social media, had actually improved company performance. A later McKinsey study did find evidence of improvement. See Jacques Bughin and Michael Chui, "The Rise of the Networked Enterprise: Web 2.0 Finds Its Payday," *McKinsey Quarterly*, December 2010.

[31] Telis Demos, "MasterCard's Keys to Survival," *Fortune*, Vol. 158, No. 8, October 27, 2008, p. 159.

Designing Robust Strategies

In some cases, the set of threats that a country or organization faces is large and the policy options are mutually exclusive because each implies a significant financial and human investment. As a result, the key policy challenge lies in finding a tool whose utility is robust across a wide range of scenarios. After the Cold War, RAND developed an approach for the U.S. Army called *assumption-based planning*. This approach identifies the key assumptions on which a current strategy is based, particularly those assumptions that are more vulnerable to changes during the strategy's time frame. It defines a series of signposts to help decisionmakers assess the relevance of initial assumptions through time. This approach allows decisionmakers to define *shaping actions*, which allow the organization to exert control over an assumption that is changing, and *hedging actions*, which are designed to limit the organization's exposure to the risk entailed by a vulnerable assumption.[32] The logic of this and kindred techniques is that if decisionmakers have a better view of the future scenarios they could face, they can gain a sense of the potential strategic modifications that they could be forced to implement in order to adapt to changes.

Examples

- **Designing and building new submarines.** This process, which can take up to 15 years, illustrates the challenge of building robust strategies. The process includes two broad phases: identifying the needed capabilities and the appropriate design and then putting the submarine together. Determining capability requires assessing the threats that a country is facing, particularly the adversary's capabilities. Once the needed capabilities have been identified, finding the appropriate design requires comparing the cost-effectiveness of different alternatives that would allow the submarines to meet the requirements. In particular, the flexibility of an alternative design and the design's ability to play a role in longer-term goals contribute to the alternative's cost-effectiveness.[33] Building a submarine fits the long-term analysis model, given the uncertainty of the threats and of the future strategic landscape, which give birth to a typical strategic dilemma.
- **Environmental policies in the context of climate uncertainty.**[34] Although climate experts are able to generate probability distributions for temperatures in the short run, deep uncertainty characterizes the weather in the long run. Standard models, past trends, and prior experience are of limited help in anticipating the future. In this context, the challenge lies in enhancing the adaptivity of environmental policies, regardless of what the future unfolds. Adaptive management plays a key role in the design of such robust policies. By defining actions in the near term and identifying signposts to monitor in the

---

[32] James A. Dewar et al., *Assumption-Based Planning: A Planning Tool for Very Uncertain Times*, Santa Monica, Calif.: RAND Corporation, MR-114-A, 1993.

[33] For a more detailed view of this process, see Office of Aerospace Studies, *Analysis Handbook—A Guide for Performing Analysis Studies: For Analysis of Alternatives or Functional Solution Analyses*, July 2004.

[34] The instances of water management under climate uncertainty and the preservation of ecosystems are particularly illustrative of this type of environmental policy. See, for instance, Robert J. Lempert and David G. Groves, "Identifying and Evaluating Robust Adaptive Policy Responses to Climate Change for Water Management Agencies in the American West," *Technological Forecasting & Social Change*, Vol. 77, 2010, pp. 960–974; Beth E. Lachman, Anny Wong, and Susan A. Resetar, *The Thin Green Line: An Assessment of DoD's Readiness and Environmental Protection Initiative to Buffer Installation Encroachment*, Santa Monica, Calif.: RAND Corporation, MG-612-OSD, 2007; David G. Groves, et al., "Planning for Climate Change in the Inland Empire: Southern California," *Water Resources IMPACT*, July 2008.

medium and longer terms, policymakers are able to better adapt to future contingencies. In particular, recent efforts to develop robust decisionmaking processes have focused on the need to use standard models and test their assumptions in different ways.[35] As in the case of the submarine, the objective in this instance is to design policies and to find tools with utility across a wide set of future scenarios.

Sometimes, decisionmakers can know with some certainty that an event will take place or a milestone will be set. Those eventualities—elections, summits, a change in the leadership of an international organization—can represent risks or opportunities. In these cases, the challenge lies in preparing for the specific events by developing hedging strategies (in the case of risks) or policies that will draw the maximum benefits (in the case of opportunities).

- **American soccer may be a useful example, if an odd one.** Although Ghana eliminated the United States in the second stage of the 2010 World Cup, the American team performed well overall. The real challenge for the U.S. Soccer Federation now is to identify opportunities and to help develop very young promising talents. The United States placed bids for hosting the World Cup—a competition in which, historically, the home-turf advantage has been considerable—in 2018 and 2022 in an effort to build the most positive environment for the young soccer talents who are likely to compete in those Cups. A related issue is determining when the U.S. Soccer Federation can change coaches without harming the team's cohesion and the coherence of the preparation efforts. In other words, identifying an opportunity, such as organizing a World Cup, is one thing, but exploiting it requires implementing a long-term strategy well before the milestone.

Hedging Against Undesirable Contingencies
Finally, strategic planning can help decisionmakers adapt to future contingencies, especially those that they fear most. That hedging against undesirable contingencies is one of the major goals of strategic analysis. Hedging strategies can be informed by theoretical and statistical models, by history and current international affairs, or, as it is most often the case, by all four.

Examples
- **Foreign exchange risk.** The European Aeronautic Defence and Space Company (EADS) is especially vulnerable to fluctuation in the euro-dollar exchange rate. As a result, EADS uses foreign exchange contracts on financial markets to hedge its future revenues and overall positions.[36] In 1999, facing the prospect of rising fuel prices likely to affect the company's operations and profits, Southwest Airlines adopted a similar approach. As of 2007, the airline owned long-term contracts on financial markets that allowed it to acquire its fuel at $51 per barrel through 2009, when the market price was around $90.[37] As a result of this strategy, in 2007 and 2008, Southwest was able to significantly increase its profits in spite of high oil prices that were causing run-ups in costs for most of the sector's strug-

---

[35] For a comprehensive view of robust decisionmaking, see Robert J. Lempert, Steven W. Popper, and Steven C. Bankes, *Shaping the Next One Hundred Years: New Methods for Quantitative, Long-Term Policy Analysis*, Santa Monica, Calif.: RAND Corporation, MR-1626-RPC, 2003.

[36] See, for instance, Peggy Hollinger, "EADS Chief Warns of Risk from Eurozone Crisis," FinancialTimes.com, May 14, 2010.

[37] Jeff Bailey, "An Airline Shrugs at Oil Prices," *New York Times*, November 29, 2007.

gling companies.[38] However, the nature and effectiveness of Southwest's strategy has been debated. First, recent drops in fuel prices point to the limits of the company's approach.[39] Second, some observers have suggested that what drove Southwest's strategy were expectations that oil prices would remain high, not a desire to reduce uncertainty—and thus the strategy was more speculation than hedging.[40] To be sure, the boundary between both approaches is blurry, but the hedge that Southwest implemented is not a substitute for good management. In particular, it is noteworthy that the firm's strategy was influenced by a narrow set of global concerns.

In the financial realm, market volatility is not just a widely documented historical feature; in theory, it also plays a useful role in providing participants with publicly available information. In this theoretical framework, participants' right to acquire options to execute a specific action in the future plays a significant role in improving the efficiency of financial markets. For instance, "puts" give the buyer the possibility to sell an underlying asset at a prespecified price, and "calls" do the same for buying an asset. In this case, the framework of free markets informs the need to protect oneself from an undesirable change in the price of an underlying asset or the ability to take a significant bet.

- **The Nuclear Non-Proliferation Treaty.** This treaty might be considered a hedge against the possible willingness of some nonnuclear powers to go nuclear. Game theory, history, and current affairs inform the debate on the theoretical efficiency of such a design. Through the treaty, the major nuclear powers, particularly the United States, seek to shape the preferences of nonnuclear powers through binding commitments that are costly to default on and through the power of example.[41] The design is an efficient hedge only as long as the strategic landscape does not affect the preferences of each actor. Although expectations about participants in the financial market are relatively easy to assess, the same is not true in international politics, especially given the significant consequences of a change in a single actor's preferences. For instance, Iran's acquisition of the potential to quickly build a nuclear weapon could be a potential tipping point in the region's strategic landscape.[42] Robust hedging strategies in international politics are all the more compli-

---

[38] Peter Pae, "Hedge on Fuel Prices Pays Off," *Los Angeles Times*, May 30, 2008; "Southwest Airlines' Fuel Hedging Pushes Profits," Associated Press, April 19, 2007.

[39] See, for instance, Justin Bachman, "Southwest Sees Fuel Hedges' Pesky Side," *Bloomberg Business Week*, October 16, 2008.

[40] Carlos Blanco, John Lehman, and Naoki Shimoda, "Hedging Strategies for Airlines: The Shareholder Value Perspective," *Air Finance Annual*, 2005.

[41] The case of Saudi Arabia is particularly interesting. One report suggests that political rather than military strategy drove Saudi Arabia's decision to sign the Nuclear Non-Proliferation Treaty in 1988. In the current context, Saudi officials realize that any change in their nuclear policy would lead the West, and specifically the United States, to give Saudi Arabia the same treatment given to Iran and North Korea. A policy shift on the part of Riyadh would entail active opposition from the United States and Israel that, according to the report, would not survive a simple cost-benefit analysis test. In addition, U.S. security guarantees to Saudi Arabia have been a fundamental incentive for Saudi Arabia to curb its nuclear programs. See Thomas Lippman, "Saudi Arabia: The Calculations of Uncertainty," in Kurt M. Campbell, Mitchell Reiss, and Robert Einhorn, eds., *The Nuclear Tipping Point: Why States Reconsider Their Nuclear Choices*, Washington, D.C.: Brookings Institution Press, 2004.

[42] See, for instance, William J. Perry and James R. Schlesinger, *America's Strategic Posture: The Final Report of the Congressional Commission on the Strategic Posture of the United States*, Washington, D.C.: United States Institute of Peace Press, May 6, 2009.

cated to design, though signposts on the evolving preferences of key actors can be identified and monitored.

- **Turkey's current "zero-problems" foreign policy, outlined by Foreign Minister Ahmet Davutoğlu.** In Minister Davutoğlu's eyes, the end of the Cold War meant that Turkey was no longer a "wing" country within NATO and that it instead needed to guarantee the Near East's stability, given Turkey's new regional status.[43] In practice, this "zero-problems" foreign policy has meant both taking note of the European Union's reluctance to admit Turkey—and thereby limiting the prospects of a direct confrontation on the topic with Brussels and European powers—and promoting a rapprochement with Iran, Syria, and the Arab world. This latter thrust has also led Ankara to reassess its relationship with Israel.[44] The prospect of never becoming a member of the European Union and of a possible decline in the European Union's relative power led Turkish authorities to hedge against the failure of Turkey's European strategy by developing a Middle Eastern strategy, which could strengthen Turkey's status as a regional leader. From this perspective, the "zero-problems" foreign policy is a hedging strategy through which Ankara seeks not only to preserve its existing options but also to exploit additional windows of opportunity.

- **Asian fiscal policies.** These policies could be considered a hedging strategy—one based on both economic theory and history. In fact, the decision to accumulate massive reserves in the wake of the Asian crisis of the late 1990s in order to be better equipped to cope with a similar crisis was not only justified from a historical point of view, given the cyclical nature of economic and financial activity; it was also grounded in Keynesian economic theory, which suggests that surpluses in expansionary periods allow economic actors, including states, to better face economic crises.[45] From this perspective, surpluses and deficits allow governments to smooth the economic cycle. In particular, surpluses in periods of economic expansion allow governments to hedge against the risk of a rapid economic downturn. The ability of some of Asian countries, such as Singapore, to face the most recent financial crisis supports the notion that the success of this hedging strategy is grounded in both theory and in history.[46]

---

[43] For a summary, see Ahmet Davutoğlu, "Turkey's Zero-Problems Foreign Policy," *Foreign Policy*, May 20, 2010.

[44] See, for instance, "Is Turkey Turning?" *The Economist*, June 10, 2010; Daniel Steinvorth, "Disillusioned with Europe, Turkey Looks East," *Der Spiegel*, December 11, 2009.

[45] In Keynes' own words,

> a decline in income due to a decline in the level of employment, if it goes far, may even cause consumption to exceed income not only by some individuals and institutions using up the financial reserves which they have accumulated in better times, but also by the Government, which will be liable, willingly or unwillingly, to run into a budgetary deficit or will provide unemployment relief; for example, out of borrowed money. Thus, when employment falls to a low level, aggregate consumption will decline by a smaller amount than that by which real income has declined, by reason both of the habitual behavior of individuals and also of the probable policy of governments; which is the explanation why a new position of equilibrium can usually be reached within a modest range of fluctuation. (John Maynard Keynes, *The General Theory of Employment, Interest and Money*, London: Macmillan Press, 1936, p. 98)

[46] See Alain Frachon, "A Singapour, rencontre avec un vrai keynésien [In Singapore, Meeting with a True Keynesian]," *Le Monde*, May 20, 2010.

The Precautionary Principle

The precautionary principle may have less relevance for foreign policy, but it does underscore the need for longer-term analysis. As the Wingspread Consensus puts it, "When an activity raises threats of harm to human health or the environment, precautionary measures should be taken even if some cause and effect relationships are not fully established scientifically."[47] The European Union has now adopted the principle as a guiding one in its decisionmaking processes.[48] Implementing the principle requires not only determining whether a strategy has reached its specific goals but also assessing the broader consequences of a policy's implementation. Therefore, in principle, the precautionary principle requires long-term analysis even if the conclusion is a very specific policy—namely, not to act but instead to sustain the status quo.

Sometimes, *not* to make a change in strategy amounts to either opting for an alternative strategy or implicitly implementing the opposite strategy. In particular, long-term analysis can justify a cautious approach to an issue and even an approach that seeks to preserve the status quo. Efforts to combat nuclear proliferation and calls for a "nuclear zero" fit this approach in the sense that the underlying analysis points to the combination of dangerous trends and broader context.[49]

The precautionary principle, especially when it is applied to domains that have the potential to harm human life or that can infringe on basic ethical principles, also corresponds to this logic. Because of their potential and hard-to-measure second-rank effects, and in spite of their potential for cures, gene therapy and cloning have, as a result of long-term analysis, been regarded with considerable caution from the scientific community.

---

[47] See, for instance, The Science and Environmental Health Network, "Wingspread Conference on the Precautionary Principle," web page, January 26, 1998.

[48] Commission of European Communities, "Communication from the Commission on the Precautionary Principle," Brussels, February 2, 2000; The European Union, The Treaty on European Union, Maastricht, February 7, 1992, Article III-233.

[49] See George P. Shultz, William J. Perry, Henry A. Kissinger, and Sam Nunn "Toward a Nuclear-Free World," *Wall Street Journal*, January 15, 2008; George P. Shultz, William J. Perry, Henry A. Kissinger, and Sam Nunn, "A World Free of Nuclear Weapons," *Wall Street Journal*, January 4, 2007. For a contrarian view, see Elbridge Colby, "Nuclear Abolition: A Dangerous Illusion," *Orbis*, Summer 2008, pp. 424–433; Harold Brown and John Deutch, "The Nuclear Disarmament Fantasy," *Wall Street Journal*, November 19, 2007.

List of Participants

Table B.1
Workshop Participants

Name	Affiliation (as of July 1, 2010)
David Aaron	RAND Corporation
Hans Binnendijk[a]	National Defense University
Daniel Byman	Georgetown University
Daniel Chiu	Office of the Secretary of Defense
Derek Chollet	Department of State
Alan Cohn	Department of Homeland Security
Peter Feaver	Duke University
Jeremy Ghez	RAND Corporation
David Gordon	Eurasia Group
Thomas Greenwood	National Security Council
Marc Grossman[a]	Cohen Group
Ryan Henry	RAND Corporation
Samuel Higgins	Office of the Secretary of Defense
Andrew Hoehn	RAND Corporation
Martin Indyk	Brookings Institution
Bruce Jentleson	Duke University and Department of State
Elizabeth Jones	APCO Worldwide
Ellen Laipson	Stimson Center
John McLaughlin	Johns Hopkins School of Advanced International Studies
Joel Meyer	Department of Homeland Security
John Negroponte	McLarty Associates
Thomas Pickering[a]	Boeing
Stapleton Roy	Wilson Center
Travis Sullivan	Department of Commerce

Table B.1—Continued

Name	Affiliation (as of July 1, 2010)
Jonathan Trexel	United States Strategic Command
Gregory Treverton	RAND Corporation
Kurt Volker	Johns Hopkins School of Advanced International Studies
Casimir Yost	Office of Director of National Intelligence

NOTE: The names of most of the Intelligence Community participants have been omitted.

[a] The participant was unable to attend the workshop but was interviewed separately.

References

Agarwal, Rajshree, and Constance E. Helfat, "Strategic Renewal of Organizations," *Organization Science*, Vol. 2, No. 2, March–April 2009, pp. 281–293.

Bachman, Justin, "Southwest Sees Fuel Hedges' Pesky Side," *Bloomberg Business Week*, October 16, 2008.

Bailey, Jeff, "An Airline Shrugs at Oil Prices," *New York Times*, November 29, 2007.

Blanco, Carlos, John Lehman, and Naoki Shimoda, "Hedging Strategies for Airlines: The Shareholder Value Perspective," *Air Finance Annual*, 2005.

Bodie, Zvi, Alex Kane, and Alan Marcus, *Investments*, New York: McGraw-Hill, 2004.

British Petroleum, "Statistical Review of World Energy," web page, June 2010. As of August 13, 2010: http://www.bp.com/statisticalreview

Brooks, David, "Prune and Go," *New York Times*, June 10, 2010.

Brown, Harold, and John Deutch, "The Nuclear Disarmament Fantasy," *Wall Street Journal*, November 19, 2007.

Bughin, Jacques, and Michael Chui, "The Rise of the Networked Enterprise: Web 2.0 Finds Its Payday," *McKinsey Quarterly*, December 2010.

Colby, Elbridge, "Nuclear Abolition: A Dangerous Illusion," *Orbis*, Summer 2008, pp. 424–433.

Commission of European Communities, "Communication from the Commission on the Precautionary Principle," Brussels, February 2, 2000.

The Commission on the Intelligence Capabilities of the United States Regarding Weapons of Mass Destruction, *Report to the President of the United States*, Washington, D.C., March 31, 2005.

Davutoğlu, Ahmet, "Turkey's Zero-Problems Foreign Policy," *Foreign Policy*, May 20, 2010.

Demos, Telis, "MasterCard's Keys to Survival," *Fortune*, Vol. 158, No. 8, October 27, 2008, p. 159.

Dewar, James A., *Assumption-Based Planning: A Tool for Reducing Avoidable Surprises*, New York: Cambridge University Press, 2002.

Dewar, James A., Carl H. Builder, William M. Hix, and Morlie Levin, *Assumption-Based Planning: A Planning Tool for Very Uncertain Times*, Santa Monica, Calif.: RAND Corporation, MR-114-A, 1993. As of July 7, 2011: http://www.rand.org/pubs/monograph_reports/MR114.html

Doshi, Viren, Hege Nordahl, and Adrian del Maestro, "Big Oil's Big Shift," Strategy-Business.com, August 2, 2010. As of July 6, 2011: http://www.strategy-business.com/article/00042?gko=62983

Drezner, Daniel W., "Bad Debts: Assessing China's Financial Influence in Great Power Politics," *International Security*, Vol. 34, No. 2, Fall 2009, pp. 7–45.

Dubner, Stephen J., "Reading, Rockets and 'Rithmetic," podcast, Freakonomics.com, October 21, 2010. As of February 18, 2011: http://freakonomics.blogs.nytimes.com/2010/10/21/freakonomics-radio-reading-rockets-and-rithmetic/

Dull, M., and P. S. Roberts, "Continuity, Competence, and the Succession of Senate-Confirmed Agency Appointees, 1989–2009," *Presidential Studies Quarterly*, Vol. 39, 2009, pp. 432–453.

Eichengreen, Barry, "Fiscal Fibs and Follies," Project-Syndicate.org, July 13, 2010. As of August 19, 2010:
http://www.project-syndicate.org/commentary/eichengreen19/English

The European Union, The Treaty on European Union, Maastricht, February 7, 1992.

Evans-Pritchard, A., "China Threatens 'Nuclear Option' of Dollar Sales," *Telegraph*, August 8, 2007.

Frachon, Alain, "A Singapour, rencontre avec un vrai keynésien [In Singapore, Meeting with a True Keynesian]," *Le Monde*, May 20, 2010.

Fryer, Bronwyn, and Thomas A. Stewart, "Cisco Sees the Future: An Interview with John Chambers," *Harvard Business Review*, November 2008, pp. 72–79.

Fuld, Leonard, "Be Prepared," *Harvard Business Review*, September 2003, pp. 20–21.

Garvin, David A., and Lynne C. Levesque, "Meeting the Challenge of Corporate Entrepreneurship," *Harvard Business Review*, Vol. 84, No. 10, pp. 102–112.

Groves, David G., et al., "Planning for Climate Change in the Inland Empire: Southern California," *Water Resources IMPACT*, July 2008.

Harreld, J. Bruce, Charles A. O'Reilly III, and Michael L. Tushman, "Dynamic Capabilities at IBM: Driving Strategy into Action," *California Management Review*, Vol. 49, No. 4, pp. 21–43.

Higgins, Robert C., *Analysis for Financial Management*, eighth edition, Boston: McGraw-Hill, 2007.

Hollinger, Peggy, "EADS Chief Warns of Risk from Eurozone Crisis," FinancialTimes.com, May 14, 2010. As of July 6, 2010:
http://www.ft.com/intl/cms/s/0/c0f0ad20-5f2c-11df-978c-00144feab49a.html#axzz1RLxI19G3

Hunter, Jackie, "Open-Source Pharmaceuticals?" Project-Syndicate.org, July 29, 2010. As of August 19, 2010:
http://www.project-syndicate.org/commentary/jhunter1/English

International Risk Governance Council, *White Paper on Risk Governance: Towards an Integrative Approach*, Geneva, 2005.

"Is Turkey Turning?" *The Economist*, June 10, 2010.

Jones, Daryl G., "Personal Savings Rate: Worse Than We Thought," Money.CNN.com, June 30, 2010. As of July 1, 2010:
http://money.cnn.com/2010/06/30/news/economy/personal_savings_decline.fortune/index.htm

Jouret, Guido, "Inside Cisco's Search for the Next Big Idea," *Harvard Business Review*, September 2009, pp. 43–45.

Keynes, John Maynard, *The General Theory of Employment, Interest and Money*, London: Macmillan Press, 1936.

Kirby, Julia, and Thomas A. Stewart, "The Institutional Yes," *Harvard Business Review*, October 2007, pp. 75–82.

Krugman, Paul, "Now and Later," *New York Times*, June 20, 2010.

Lachman, Beth E., Anny Wong, and Susan A. Resetar, *The Thin Green Line: An Assessment of DoD's Readiness and Environmental Protection Initiative to Buffer Installation Encroachment*, Santa Monica, Calif.: RAND Corporation, MG-612-OSD, 2007. As of July 7, 2011:
http://www.rand.org/pubs/monographs/MG612.html

Lempert, Robert J., and David G. Groves, "Identifying and Evaluating Robust Adaptive Policy Responses to Climate Change for Water Management Agencies in the American West," *Technological Forecasting & Social Change*, Vol. 77, 2010, pp. 960–974.

Lempert, Robert J., Steven W. Popper, and Steven C. Bankes, *Shaping the Next One Hundred Years: New Methods for Quantitative, Long-Term Policy Analysis*, Santa Monica, Calif.: RAND Corporation, MR-1626-RPC, 2003. As of July 7, 2011:
http://www.rand.org/pubs/monograph_reports/MR1626.html

Leonard, David, "The New Abnormal," BusinessWeek.com, July 29, 2010. As of August 19, 2010: http://www.businessweek.com/magazine/content/10_32/b4190050473272.htm

Lesser, Ian, "Turkey, Brazil, & Iran: A Glimpse of the Future," *Real Clear Politics*, May 21, 2010.

Lippman, Thomas, "Saudi Arabia: The Calculations of Uncertainty," in Kurt M. Campbell, Mitchell Reiss, and Robert Einhorn, eds., *The Nuclear Tipping Point: Why States Reconsider Their Nuclear Choices*, Washington, D.C.: Brookings Institution Press, 2004.

McKay, Betsy, and Robert Guth, "Global AIDS Fight Shifts Toward Prevention," *Wall Street Journal*, July 17, 2010.

Nocera, Joe, "Risk Mismanagement," *New York Times*, January 4, 2009.

Nye, Jr., Joseph S., "Peering into the Future," *Foreign Affairs*, Vol. 77, No. 4, July/August 1994, pp. 82–93.

Office of Aerospace Studies, *Analysis Handbook—A Guide for Performing Analysis Studies: For Analysis of Alternatives or Functional Solution Analyses*, July 2004.

Pae, Peter, "Hedge on Fuel Prices Pays Off," *Los Angeles Times,* May 30, 2008.

Panza, G. F., K. Irikura, M. Kouteva, A. Peresan, Z. Wang, and R. Saragoni, "Advanced Seismic Hazard Assessment," *Pure and Applied Geophysics*, Vol. 168, August 4, 2010, pp. 1–9.

Perry, William J., and James R. Schlesinger, *America's Strategic Posture: The Final Report of the Congressional Commission on the Strategic Posture of the United States*, Washington, D.C.: United States Institute of Peace Press, 2009.

The Pew Global Attitudes Project, "Obama More Popular Abroad Than at Home, Global Image of U.S. Continues to Benefit," web page, June 17, 2010. As of July 13, 2010: http://pewglobal.org/2010/06/17/obama-more-popular-abroad-than-at-home/

RAND Corporation, "Database of Worldwide Terrorism Incidents," web page, no date available. As of October 20, 2010: http://www.rand.org/nsrd/projects/terrorism-incidents

The Science and Environmental Health Network, "Wingspread Conference on the Precautionary Principle," web page, January 26, 1998. As of August 16, 2010: http://www.sehn.org/wing.html

Science Daily, "New Building Design Withstands Earthquake Simulation," web page, March 9, 2009. As of August 13, 2010: http://www.sciencedaily.com/releases/2009/02/090227080558.htm

Shell, "What Are Scenarios?" web page, undated. As of August 13, 2010: http://www.shell.com/home/content/aboutshell/our_strategy/shell_global_scenarios/what_are_scenarios/

Shell International BV, *Energy Scenarios to 2050*, 2008.

Shultz, George P., William J. Perry, Henry A. Kissinger, and Sam Nunn, "A World Free of Nuclear Weapons," *Wall Street Journal*, January 4, 2007.

———, "Toward a Nuclear-Free World," *Wall Street Journal*, January 15, 2008.

Skidelsky, Robert, "Keynes Versus the Classics: Round Two," Project-Syndicate.org, October 10, 2009. As of August 19, 2010: http://www.project-syndicate.org/commentary/skidelsky22/English

Society of Petroleum Engineers, *Glossary of Terms Used in Petroleum Reserves and Resources Definitions*, undated.

"Southwest Airlines' Fuel Hedging Pushes Profits," Associated Press, April 19, 2007.

Steinvorth, Daniel, "Disillusioned with Europe, Turkey Looks East," *Der Spiegel*, December 11, 2009.

Sull, Donald N., "Strategy as Active Waiting," *Harvard Business Review*, September 2005, pp. 120–129.

Summers, Lawrence, "Reflections on Global Account Imbalances and Emerging Markets Reserve Accumulation," speech, Reserve Bank of India, Mumbai, March 24, 2006.

Sutter, John D., "In Search of an Earthquake-Proof Building," CNN.com, March 2, 2010. As of August 13, 2010:
http://www.cnn.com/2010/TECH/03/02/earthquake.resistant.building/index.html

Treverton, Gregory F., "Estimating Beyond the Cold War," *Defense Intelligence Journal*, Vol. 3, No. 2, Fall 1994.

———, *Next Steps in Reshaping Intelligence*, Santa Monica, Calif.: RAND Corporation, OP-152-RC, 2005. As of July 7, 2011:
http://www.rand.org/pubs/occasional_papers/OP152.html

Treverton, Gregory F., and C. Bryan Gabbard, *Assessing the Tradecraft of Intelligence Analysis*, Santa Monica, Calif.: RAND Corporation, TR-293, 2008.

Tuner, Aider, "The Uses and Abuses of Economic Ideology," Project-Syndicate.org, July 15, 2010. As of August 8, 2010:
http://www.project-syndicate.org/commentary/turner1/English

Watson, Ivan, and Mitra Mobasherat, "Turkey: Iran Nuclear Swap Offer Shows 'Vision,'" CNN.com, May 18, 2010. As of August 19, 2010:
http://www.cnn.com/2010/WORLD/europe/05/18/iran.nuclear/index.html

Vincent, Catherine, "Au Cameroun, la décentralisation du traitement contre le VIH est efficace [In Cameroon, Decentralizing the Fight Against AIDS Is Efficient]," *Le Monde*, August 14, 2010.